First Lessor
Bongo

by Trevor Salloum

© Cover photo courtesy of Latin Percussion

Online Audio   www.melbay.com/30045BCDEB

1 2

Visit us on the Web at www.melbay.com — E-mail us at email@melbay.com

CONTENTS

ABOUT THE AUTHOR

Trevor Salloum is well known internationally as a music educator who specializes in Afro-Cuban and Middle Eastern drumming. He has taught drumming at universities, colleges and schools for over 30 years. He studied music at Notre Dame University, the Banff School of Fine Arts and York University. He is a best selling author with Mel Bay Publications Inc. and has produced numerous books, CDs, DVDs and videos on drumming.

INTRODUCTION

First Lessons® Bongo is designed as an introduction to bongo drumming for the complete novice. This book will help get you started with the fundamentals to create exciting rhythms. You will learn correct posture, hand positions, music terminology, drum strokes, exercises and basic rhythms. I hope you will enjoy exploring the rich and fascinating world of bongo drumming.

ACKNOWLEDGEMENTS

I would like to thank my family, friends, teachers, Armando Peraza, José Mangual Sr., Jack Costanzo, Candido Camero, Tomás Cruz, Israel "Toto" Berriel, Changuito, Giovanni Hidalgo, Rebeca Mauleon, John Santos, Memo Acevedo, Michael Spiro, the staff at Mel Bay Publications, LP Music Group and Regal Tip Sticks. I am grateful to my dear friends and colleagues Tricia Dalgleish and Francisco Jaramillo for proofreading and editing the text. Thank you to Josh Buck (Mel Bay Publications), Nori Wentworth (Wentworth Music) and Peter Lafferty (Roland Canada) for audio advice. I would like to convey a heart felt thank you to my son, Gabriel Salloum, for assisting with the photography.

WEB RESOURCES

www.trevorsalloum.com
www.melbay.com

ENDORSEMENTS

www.lpmusicgroup.com
www.regaltip.com

Email questions or comments to:
rhythmproject@gmail.com

MEL BAY PUBLICATIONS BY TREVOR SALLOUM

The Bongo Book (Book/Audio) 1997 ISBN 0-7866-2071-4
Fun with Bongos (Book/Audio) 1999 ISBN 978-0786661381
Bongo Drumming (Book/Audio) 2000 ISBN 0-7866-4384-6
Afro-Latin Polyrhythms (Book/Audio) 2001 ISBN 0-7866-5422-8
Afro-Cuban Rhythms Vol.1 (Booklet) 2004 ISBN 0-7866-7253-6
Afro-Cuban Rhythms Vol.2 (Booklet) 2004 ISBN 0-7866-7254-4
The Art of Bongo Drumming (DVD) 2006
The Art of Arabic Drumming (DVD) 2007
Afro-Cuban Percussion (Booklet/Audio) 2009 ISBN 978-078667948-5
The School of Bongo (Book/Audio) 2011 ISBN 978-078668273-7
First Lessons Conga (Book/Audio) 2012 ISBN 978-078-668-449-6

DESCRIPTION

The bongo drum consists of two single-headed, cylindrical shells separated by a bridge. The smaller, higher-pitched drum is called the *macho* (male) and the larger, lower-pitched drum is the called the *hembra* (female). The shells and bridge are usually made of wood or fiberglass. The heads are derived from animal hide (cow, goat, mule) although synthetic plastic heads are becoming more common. The tension of the head is adjusted by metal tuning rods (lugs) that attach to a circular metal rim on the top and bottom of the shell. The top rim applies pressure to a wire ring that is tucked into the hide. A nut that is located below the bottom rim allows the lugs to be tightened. The shells are about 6.5 inches in height and head diameters are approximately 7 inches for the *macho* and 8.5 inches for the *hembra*.

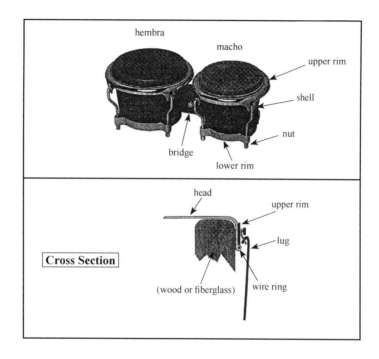

HISTORY

The bongo drum has a rich history that is thought to have begun in the mid-1800s in Cuba. Originally, the bongos were the only drums used in the early *son* style of music. This music was mostly a rural style that required a certain amount of portability especially when played by travelling military.

Son is not only the ancestor of salsa, but rock and roll as well. Eventually, the bongos migrated to the cities and were used in most forms of popular dance music. In the 1920-30s some of the *son* groups (Sexteto Habanero, Septeto Nacional, etc.) travelled to perform in the United States. Many of these recordings have been reissued and are readily available. The influences of the bongos began pervading into other styles of music. The popular bands of Xavier Cugat, Perez Prado, Machito, Stan Kenton, Woody Herman and Don Aziapu all utilized bongos in their music. Prominent *bongoceros* (bongo drummers) of the 1930-50s began making their mark in history including Augustin Gutierrez, Pedro Mena, Chino Pozo, Anolin "Papa Kila" Suarez, José Mangual Sr., Armando Peraza, Mongo Santamaria, Jack Costanzo, Candido Camero, Sabu Martinez and Ray Romero.

In the 1950s the bongo drum became more popular with the advent of "bongo parties," bongo contests and the development of the beat generation.

Bongos continue to experience popularity in adding flavor to various genres of music and are now used throughout classical, rock, flamenco, jazz, Latin, Middle Eastern and East Indian music.

NOTATION KEY

Notes for the bongo drum are usually arranged on the musical staff in order of pitch. Notes of the *hembra* are placed lower on the staff. Notes of the *macho* are placed higher on the staff.

There are two common ways to notate bongo rhythms. One method is the *Cuban* approach, which utilizes various symbol note heads to indicate the type of stroke being played. For example, an X enclosed by a circle represents the fingertips. The second approach, which I will call the *East Coast* style, maintains the common black dot note head for all strokes, but indicates the particular stroke by an initial above or below the note (O=open, M=muted, etc.). Both methods have their advantages and disadvantages. The *Cuban* style has less text on the page, but the reader must refer to a legend until the symbols are memorized. The *East Coast* method has more text on a page, which may appear cluttered, but is easier to learn quickly. In this book, I have chosen to use the *East Coast* approach.

POSTURE/POSITIONING

The bongo drum can be played while sitting or standing. In both positions a metal stand can be used to hold the drum. The traditional method is to hold the drum between the inside of the knees while seated. Drummers who play multiple percussion instruments may find the standing position easier for maneuvering between instruments.

While seated, place the drum between your knees and slightly tilted away from you. The *hembra* is placed on your right side and the *macho* is placed to your left (if right-handed). This positioning may be reversed for left-handed players.

The arms are bent at about a 45° angle at the inside of the elbows. The underside of the wrists and forearms may rest on the thighs while playing.

The feet should be placed flat on the floor with the right foot almost perpendicular to the left foot. This will help place the *macho* slightly higher than the *hembra* and facilitate playing the bongo patterns.

The back and neck should be relatively erect with all limbs being relaxed. Try to envision a string being attached to your head while lifting the head up and away from the body.

At the first sign of pain or discomfort stop and reevaluate your position/posture. Stretching once you have warmed up can also help prevent injuries.

The most important aspects to drumming are posture and breathing. Breathe steadily and deeply from the diaphragm first and then the chest. Try to keep the whole body relaxed, especially the fingers, hands, arms and shoulders.

TUNING

The earliest bongos had tacked heads and were tuned with heat sources such as an open flame or applying friction. The tacked heads posed numerous problems as the pitch of the skin changed dramatically, with changes in weather. In addition, *bongoceros* would often burn their drumheads with the open flame.

The introduction of metal tuning hardware solved many problems for the *bongocero* and expedited the tuning process. There are typically four tuning lugs on the *macho* and four on the *hembra*. Each drum is tuned by tightening the metal nut on the bottom of the lug, progressing clockwise, using an equal amount of torque. Periodically check the distance between the top of the head and the rim to make sure there is uniform tension, otherwise it is very difficult to correct a slanted head in the future. The *macho* is usually tuned between a 5th to an octave higher than the *hembra* although many *bongoceros* do not intentionally tune to specific notes.

It is generally recommended to slacken off the tension of the *macho* when finished playing, especially if you don't plan to use the drums for a few days. This will prevent the heads from wearing out prematurely due to the extreme tension of the *macho*. The *hembra* doesn't need to be loosened unless you are shipping them or not playing for a few weeks. For a comprehensive description of head replacement and subsequent tuning see *The Bongo Book*, Mel Bay Publications 1997.

STROKES

Throughout the text, we indicate the striking pattern for those who are right hand dominant. Left hand dominant players will generally reverse the striking patterns. Most rhythm notation will indicate the right hand only (R). You can assume any unlabeled notes will be played with the left hand.

In the following pages, these letters will indicate which stroke is played: O=open, M=muted, S=slap, T=Toe, H=Heel, m=muff. When no letters appear beneath a note, you can assume this means to play an open stroke.

The open stroke can be played with the fingertips or up to half the palm depending on the intent.

In the *martillo* (main bongo rhythm) the *bongocero* will use the fingertips, but in soloing or for greater volume, the larger surface area including the palm is often used.

When playing the muted stroke the right hand has several striking options. You can use 1) all fingers in unison 2) index finger 3) middle finger or 4) alternate between index and middle fingers.

In bongo drumming, we use two main slaps; the closed slap and open slap. The closed slap is played with the fingertips (2nd-5th fingers) together while bracing the heel on the drum edge. The open slap is played with the same part of the hand as the closed slap except that the fingers bounce off the head. The slaps and the muff are primarily used for soloing.

STROKE LEGEND

O

All strokes in this book will usually appear with the standard music notehead and letters below designating the type of stroke. This example shows an open quarter note played on the macho.

The Open Stroke (O) is played with 1-4 fingers or the palm of the hand. Start with the hand raised off the drumhead at a 45-90 degree angle from the drumhead. The fingers strike between the edge and the center of the drumhead. The fingers rebound off the drumhead.

The Muff Stroke (m) begins the same as the Open Stroke. It is executed by striking the drum surface with almost the full length of the fingers, but no palm. The striking hand does not rebound.

The Slap Strokes (S) are both played by striking the drum surface with the fingertips while bracing the heel of the hand on the edge of the drumhead. The slap is started in a similar manner as the Open Stroke. For the **Closed Slap** there is also no rebound. **The Open Slap** is played exactly the same way as the closed slap, but the striking fingers rebound off the drumhead.

 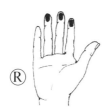
L   R

The Muted Stroke (M) is played by lightly pressing the left thumb and thenar eminence (fat pad below the thumb) against the head while striking with the right finger(s).

L

MANOTEO (Heel Toe Movement)

Heel (H) or **Thumb Strike** is played by simultaeously striking the left thumb and thenar eminence against the drumhead.

L

Toe (T) or **Finger Strike** is played by tapping the left fingertips at the center of the drumhead. It can also be played by sweeping the palm of the left hand across the drumhead towards the right hand.

Photos of Bongo Strokes

Starting Position   **Finished Position**

Muted (martillo downbeats 1, 3)

Toe (martillo upbeats 1+, 3+)

Open (martillo downbeat 2)

Heel (martillo upbeats 2+)

Open (martillo downbeat 4)

Heel (martillo upbeat 4+)

Muff

Closed Slap

Open Slap

Music Notation 1

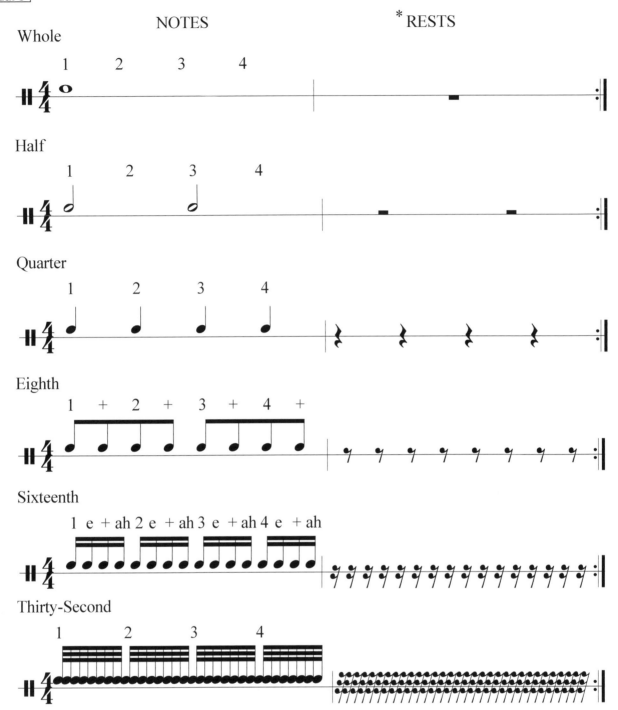

*A rest indicates the beat is silent for the value of the rest. It is still counted but not played.
A dot after a note or rest indicates an added value of one half the rest or note which precedes it.
When two notes are tied together the last note of the tie is interpreted as a rest.

Music Notation 2

SIXTEENTH NOTE VARIATIONS

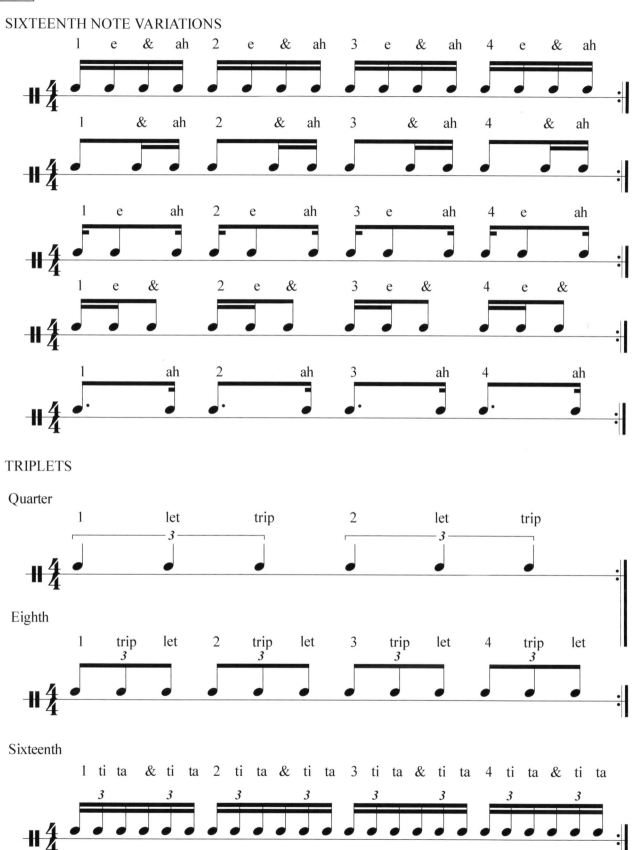

TRIPLETS

Quarter

Eighth

Sixteenth

Music Terminology

A music staff is typically composed of five lines and four spaces, each representing a different pitch/tone. In this text we will use a 1-line staff since we are using two drums. The *macho* (higher pitch) is above the line and the *hembra* (lower pitch) is below.

Macho
Hembra

Vertical bar lines divide the staff into smaller subunits of music called measures or bars.

measure 1   measure 2

A time signature at the beginning of the staff indicates the value of each measure. In 4/4 time each measure has a value equal to four quarter notes per measure. The top number indicates "how many," while the bottom number indicates "what type of notes."

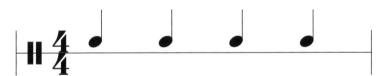

This measure would be counted "1, 2, 3, 4" in 4/4 time. It is also called *Common time* which is indicated by a large C at the beginning of the staff.

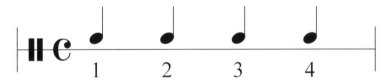

1   2   3   4

Cut time occurs in many forms of dance music and is indicated by putting a vertical line through the C. Instead of counting 1, 2, 3, 4 you would count "1 and 2 and."

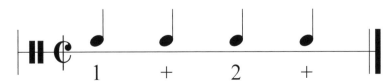

1   +   2   +

Music Terminology 2

Odd numbers of notes grouped together usually appear with a number above, indicating the number of notes in the group.

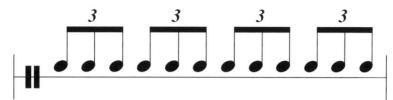

Accents are indicated by the "greater than" symbol (>). These notes are given greater than usual emphasis and are played louder.

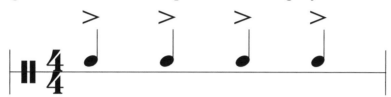

Standard repeat signs consist of two dots placed central to double bar lines. Everything within the repeat symbols is repeated one or more times.

A diagonal line dividing two dots in the center of a measure, means to repeat the proceeding measure.

When this sign bisects a bar line it suggests repeating the two previous measures.

General Warm Ups 1

Single Stroke Roll

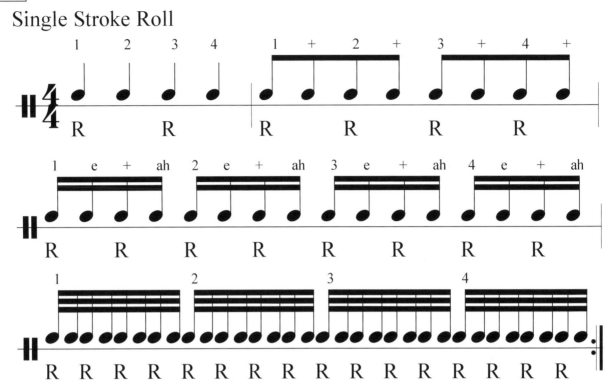

Notes that fall on the numbers 1, 2, 3, 4 are called "downbeats". Notes that fall between the downbeats 1+, 2+, 3+, 4+ are called "upbeats".

Double Stroke Roll

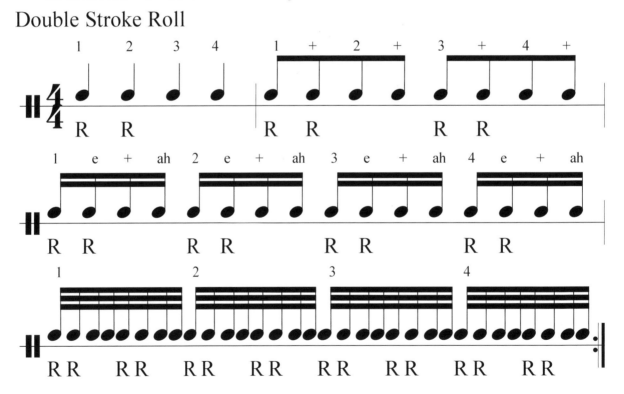

Warm Ups can be played on either the macho or the hembra. Try to count each pattern while playing. When counting 32nd notes it is much easier to only count the downbeats 1, 2, 3, 4.

General Warm Ups 2

Triplets A

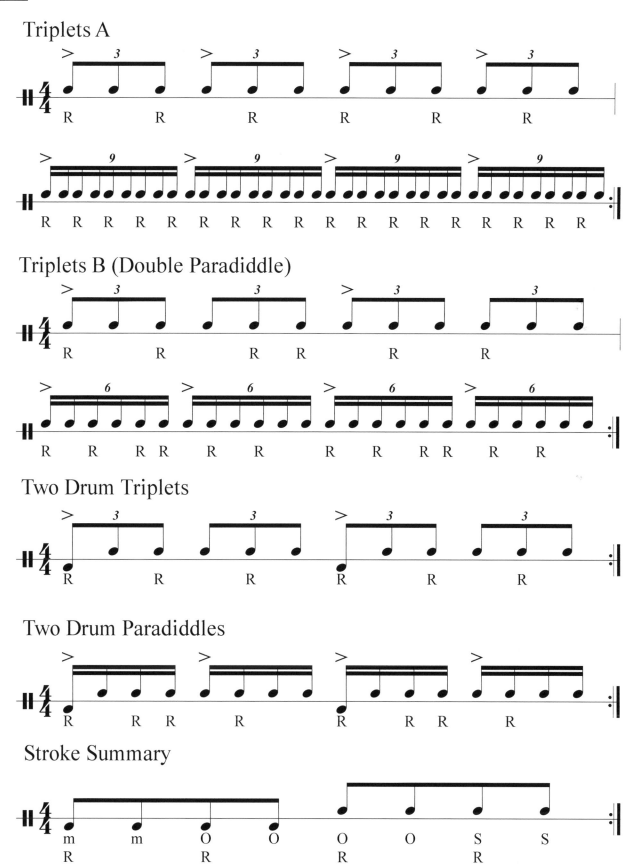

Triplets B (Double Paradiddle)

Two Drum Triplets

Two Drum Paradiddles

Stroke Summary

Slaps (S) can be played as a Closed or Open Slap.

15

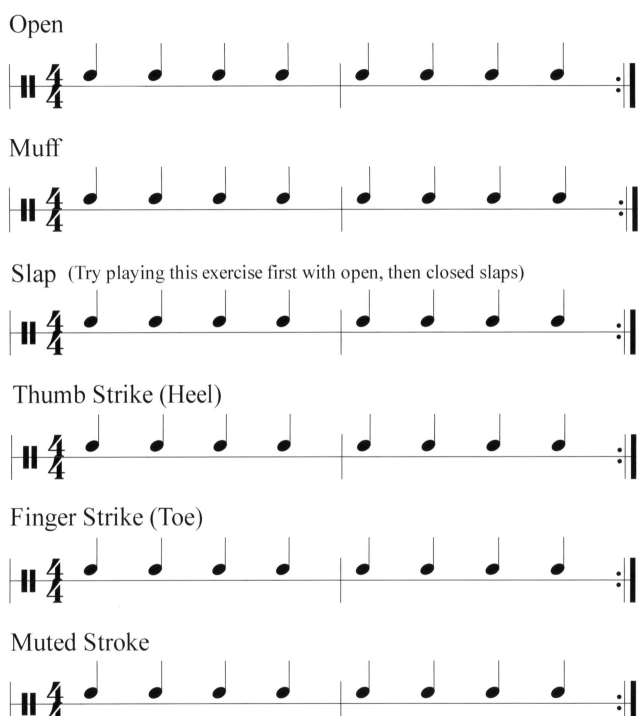

Bongo Exercises 1

Play each exercise line slowly (60 bpm). The first three exercies can be played with either hand.

Open

Muff

Slap (Try playing this exercise first with open, then closed slaps)

Thumb Strike (Heel)

Finger Strike (Toe)

Muted Stroke

Bongo Exercises 2

Play each exercise slowly (60 bpm). All patterns on this page are played with open strokes

1 4/4 R   R   R   R

2 4/4 R   R   R   R

3 4/4 R   R   R   R

4 4/4 R   R   R   R

Bongo Exercises 3

Play each exercise slowly (60 bpm). All patterns on this page are played with open strokes

1

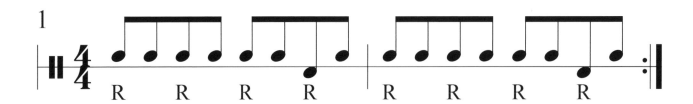

2

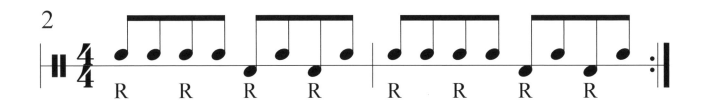

3

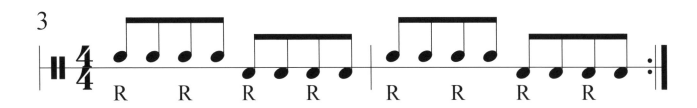

4

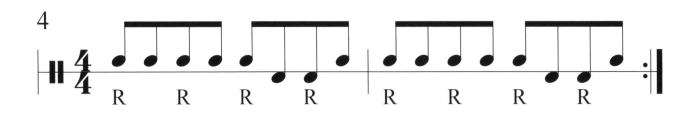

CLAVE

Clave (pronounced cláh-vay) is derived from the word "key" in Spanish. The clave is both an instrument and a rhythmic pattern. It is the foundation of most Afro-Cuban music. The clave consists of two hardwood sticks that are roughly 8 inches long by 1 inch in diameter. The larger one is called the *hembra* and the smaller the *macho*.

The hand position is very important in order to get the precise sound. The *hembra* is held in the non-dominant hand and propped up with the thumb on one side and the fingers along the other side of the stick. The cupping of the palm below the stick creates a hollow sound chamber. The dominant hand holds the macho and strikes the *hembra* in the middle of the stick to create the sound. (See photo on Clave Positioning)

There are two main clave patterns, *Son Clave* and *Rumba Clave*. *Son Clave* is the oldest and the most commonly used in popular music. It is named after the *son* style of music from Eastern Cuba. *Rumba Clave* is used primarily in rumba, but may be used in some popular styles as well (Songo, Mozambique, etc.). Both patterns consist of 5 notes in a two bar phrase, usually notated in 4/4 time. The bar with 3 notes is often called the "3 side" and the bar with 2 notes is called the "2 side." In *Son Clave* the notes are played on the 1, 2+, 4 (3 side) and on the 2, 3 (2 side). In *Rumba Clave* the notes are played on the 1, 2+, 4+ (3 side) and on the 2, 3 (2 side). The bar with the three notes is the most syncopated (contains upbeats) and creates a sense of movement/tension. The bar with the two notes (both downbeats) creates a sense of stability/relaxation.

In Cuba, clave is typically written as a one bar phrase with sixteenth notes, instead of a two bar phrase with eighth notes.

The clave pattern is important in stating the rhythmic phrasing within the musical piece. Often the clave is determined after the song has been written. The composer will determine which way the clave fits best, but most salsa songs are in 2/3 clave.

All instruments in the ensemble are required to be in correct alignment with the clave. Although the clave instrument may not be played in every song, it is implied in the phrasing of all the musicians, especially the percussionists. The cascara or paila ("shell") pattern may be used to outline the clave when the clave is absent. The pattern is played in rumba on the gua-gua (mounted piece of bamboo) or shell of the conga drum and split between two hands. The pattern is typically played in popular Latin music with one hand. It can be played on the shell of the timbale, the cowbell, the block, or the cymbal, while the other hand plays a supportive pattern.

Throughout the book, clave direction, 3/2 or 2/3, may be indicated above the staff. If no clave direction is suggested, then either clave direction could work.

CLAVE POSITIONING

Son Clave

3/2 Son Clave

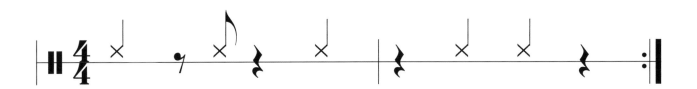

2/3 Son Clave

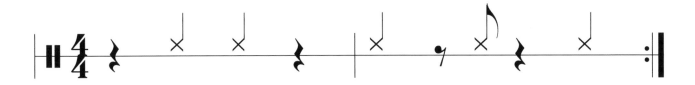

Martillo Basic with Fill: 3/2 clave alignment

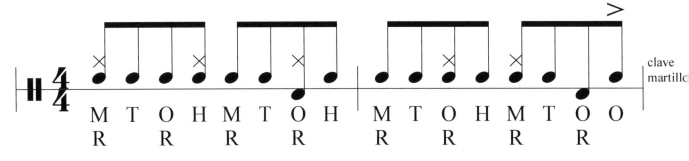

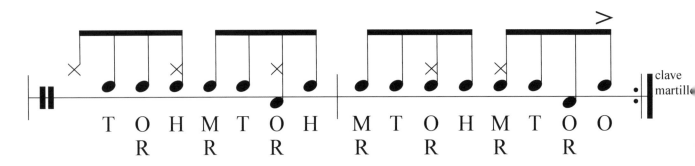

BONGO BELL

The bongo bell (*cencerro*, *campana*) is a descendant of the hoe blade (*guataca*) that is used in Afro-Cuban folkloric music. In the Latin orchestra the *bongocero* will often switch between playing the bongo and the bongo bell. The bell is held in the non-dominant hand and struck by the dominant hand as show in the photo. There are two main tones—an open (o) and a higher-pitched closed tone (c). A third high tone can also be played on the edge. Variations in tone can also be achieved by muffling the bell with the left hand/fingers. The bongo bell is generally reserved for the *Montuno* (call and response) section of music where greater drive and volume is needed. There are two primary bell patterns that the *bongocero* can play as notated below.

Track 11

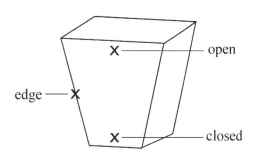

C - closed end or edge of cowbell
O - open

Basic

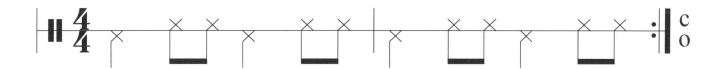

Variation 2/3 Clave

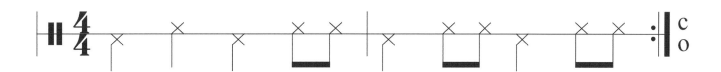

MARTILLO

The *martillo* and its variations are primary rhythms played on the bongo drum in popular forms of Afro-Cuban music (*Son, Son Montuno, Guaracha, Mambo, Salsa, Bachata, Bolero* etc.). The pattern will often only vary in speed between the musical styles, although each will have its own characteristics (see musical notation for examples). *Martillo* means hammer in Spanish. The repetitive sound of eighth notes gives the impression of a tapping hammer. The *bongocero* compliments the *conguero* as a timekeeper, but has more freedom to weave in and out of the musical piece, creating flavor to the sound.

Observe your hand positions to make sure you:
1. Keep the left thumb on the macho for the muted stroke. This is labeled as "M"
2. Remove the left hand from the playing surface for making the open tone (O).
3. Relax the thumbs of both hands so they are not tense.
4. Use the correct part of the palm to make the open tone (anywhere from the fingertips to the middle of the palm depending of the intent)

MARTILLO FILLS

Fills are short breaks within the *martillo* structure or riffs that extend for a few bars. They are short phrases of improvisation that can be used for a break in the rhythm or to start or end a passage. When they exist for more than a few bars we would consider them a solo. When playing fills it is important to maintain the musical style and tempo. The *martillo* fills presented here are a few examples that are incorporated in the *martillo* pattern. The possibilities are endless.

SOLOING

Drummers use many different ideas when soloing. Solos may involve several bars of improvisation or extend for numerous bars.

The improvisation for a solo may be simple with few open strokes and basic patterns (rudiments such as rolls, paradiddles and triplets) or complex with various strokes, advanced rudiments, polyrhythms (multiple rhythms at the same time) and syncopation (accenting upbeats). More important than technical prowess, is creating a solo that is pleasing to the ear. An extended solo should tell a story by starting simply and developing a theme, building up to a climax and then a conclusion. It should demonstrate some continuity throughout, rather than be a string of separate ideas. It is very important that the soloist is aware of the clave and uses phrasing that compliments the clave direction. Listen to some of the great *bongoceros* listed in the *History* section and then create your own solos. Play along with the metronome or clave tracks. In time you will be making great music and above all, having fun.

Martillo 1

*Before playing the Muted Stroke (M) place the left thumb in position against the drumhead as in the Heel Stroke (H)

Part A

M T O H M T O H M T O H M T O H
R R R R R R R R

Part B

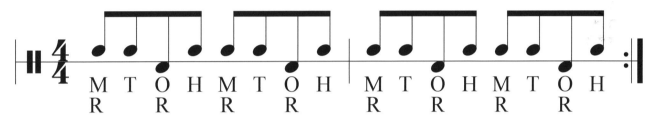

M T O H M T O H M T O H M T O H
R R R R R R R R

Basic Martillo

M T O H M T O H M T O H M T O H
R R R R R R R R

Variation

M T O H M T O H M T O H M T O H
R R R R R R R R

Martillo 2

Variations

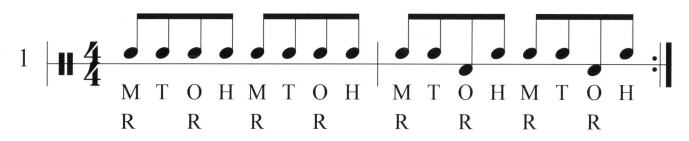

1 | 4/4 M T O H M T O H | M T O H M T O H :||
       R   R   R   R   R   R   R   R

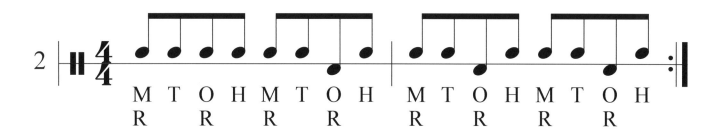

2 | 4/4 M T O H M T O H | M T O H M T O H :||
       R   R   R   R   R   R   R   R

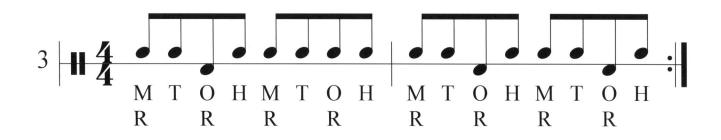

3 | 4/4 M T O H M T O H | M T O H M T O H :||
       R   R   R   R   R   R   R   R

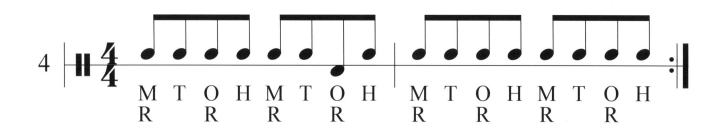

4 | 4/4 M T O H M T O H | M T O H M T O H :||
       R   R   R   R   R   R   R   R